ANIMALES AFRICANOS/AFRICAN ANIMALS
Suricatos/Meerkats

por/by Jody Sullivan Rake

Traducción/Translation: Dr. Martín Luis Guzmán Ferrer
Editor consultor/Consulting Editor: Dra. Gail Saunders-Smith

Consultor/Consultant: George Wittemyer, PhD
NSF International Postdoctoral Fellow
University of California at Berkeley

Capstone press®

Mankato, Minnesota

Pebble Plus is published by Capstone Press,
151 Good Counsel Drive, P.O. Box 669, Mankato, Minnesota 56002.
www.capstonepress.com

1 2 3 4 5 6 14 13 12 11 10 09

Library of Congress Cataloging-in-Publication Data
Rake, Jody Sullivan.
  [Meerkats. Spanish & English]
  Suricatos = Meerkats / por/by Jodie Sullivan Rake.
  p. cm. — (Animales africanos = African animals)
  Includes index.
  Summary: "Discusses meerkats, their African habitat, food, and behavior — in both English and Spanish" —
Provided by publisher.
  ISBN-13: 978-1-4296-3264-5 (hardcover)
  ISBN-10: 1-4296-3264-X (hardcover)
   1. Meerkat — Africa — Juvenile literature. I. Title. II. Title: Meerkats. III. Series.
QL737.C235R3518 2009
599.74'2 — dc22   2008034547

Editorial Credits
Erika L. Shores, editor; Katy Kudela, bilingual editor; Adalín Torres-Zayas, Spanish copy editor;
    Renée T. Doyle, designer; Laura Manthe, photo researcher

Photo Credits
Afripics.com, 14–15, 18–19
Art Life Images/David Paynter, 12–13
Bruce Coleman Inc./Clem Haagner, 20–21
iStockphoto/Jacynth Roode, cover; Nico Smit, 8–9; Peter Malsbury, 1; xyno, 22
Shutterstock/EcoPrint, 6–7, 16–17; Nicola Gavin, cover, 1, 3 (fur), 10–11
SuperStock Inc./ZSSD, 5

Note to Parents and Teachers

The Animales africanos/African Animals set supports national science standards related
to life science. This book describes and illustrates meerkats in both English and Spanish.
The images support early readers in understanding the text. The repetition of words and
phrases helps early readers learn new words. This book also introduces early readers
to subject-specific vocabulary words, which are defined in the Glossary section. Early
readers may need assistance to read some words and to use the Table of Contents,
Glossary, Internet Sites, and Index sections of the book.

Table of Contents

Tabla de contenidos

Living in Africa

Meerkats live in Africa.

They play in the sun.

They rest in the shade.

La vida en África

Los suricatos viven en África.

Les gusta jugar al sol.

Descansan en la sombra.

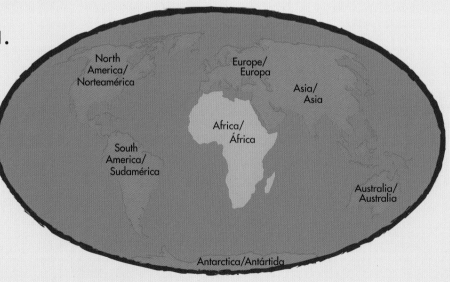

World Map/Mapamundi

Some meerkats live on grassy savannas. Other meerkats live on dry plains.

Algunos suricatos viven en sabanas llenas de pasto. Otros suricatos viven en planicies áridas.

Map of Africa/
Mapa de África

█ where meerkats live/
lugares donde viven suricatos

Up Close!

Meerkats stand up straight on their hind legs. They look for danger all around.

¡De cerca!

Los suricatos se paran en sus patas traseras. Ven si hay peligro en los alrededores.

Meerkats use sharp claws
to dig burrows. They also
dig for food.

Los suricatos usan sus
filosas garras para excavar
madrigueras. También excavan
para buscar comida.

Eating

Meerkats eat bugs, reptiles, and small rodents. What a creepy crawly meal!

La comida

Los suricatos comen insectos, reptiles y roedores pequeños. ¡Que almuerzo tan asqueroso y horrendo!

Water is often hard to find
where meerkats live. They get
water from the food they eat.

Muchas veces es difícil encontrar
agua donde viven los suricatos.
El agua la sacan de lo que comen.

Staying Safe

There is safety in numbers.

Meerkats live together

in mobs.

Estar a salvo

Hay mayor seguridad si son

muchos. Los suricatos viven

en grandes manadas.

One meerkat stays behind while
the mob hunts. The meerkat
babysitter watches over the pups.

Un suricato se queda en casa
mientras la manada caza.
El suricato nodriza cuida
a los cachorros.

Meerkats bark to warn the mob
of predators. Meerkats run to their
burrows to hide underground.
Stay safe, meerkats!

Los suricatos ladran para advertirles
a los demás que hay predadores.
Corren a su madriguera para
esconderse bajo tierra.
¡Pónganse a salvo, suricatos!

Glossary

burrow — a tunnel or hole in the ground made or used by an animal

mob — a group of meerkats that live together

plains — open land with few trees

predator — an animal that hunts other animals for food; eagles and jackals hunt meerkats.

pup — a young meerkat

reptile — a cold-blooded animal that breathes air and has a backbone; most reptiles have scaly skin.

rodent — a small mammal with long front teeth

savanna — a flat, grassy plain with few trees

Glosario

el cachorro — suricato joven

la madriguera — túnel o agujero en la tierra que hace o usa un animal

la manada — gran grupo de suricatos que viven juntos

la planicie — espacio abierto con pocos árboles

el predador — animal que caza otros animales para obtener comida; las águilas y las hienas cazan suricatos.

el reptil — animal de sangre fría que respira aire y tiene columna vertebral

el roedor — mamífero pequeño con dientes frontales alargados

la sabana — planicie con pasto y pocos árboles

Internet Sites

FactHound offers a safe, fun way to find educator-approved Internet sites related to this book.

Here's what you do:
1. Visit *www.facthound.com*
2. Choose your grade level.
3. Begin your search.

This book's ID number is 9781429632645.

FactHound will fetch the best sites for you!

Sitios de Internet

FactHound te brinda una forma segura y divertida de encontrar sitios de Internet relacionados con este libro y aprobados por docentes.

Lo haces así:
1. Visita *www.facthound.com*
2. Selecciona tu grado escolar.
3. Comienza tu búsqueda.

El número de identificación de este libro es 9781429632645.

¡FactHound buscará los mejores sitios para ti!

Index

Índice